FUN CARTOONS FOR
TRUMP PROTESTERS

Edited by Ron Coleman

Introduction

Almost three million more people voted against Donald Trump than voted for him, but because our elections are decided by an Electoral College system, he won the office. There is a lot of speculation that the win was not legitimate because of interference by the Russian government and by actions of FBI Director James Comey. The country has seen an incredible amount of chaos since Mr. Trump's election and protest movements have broken out everywhere, not only in this country but worldwide.

At the time of this writing, a poll by Public Policy Polling finds Mr. Trump's approval rate dropping precipitously. In their first poll Americans were evenly divided on Trump with 44% approving of him and 44% disapproving. After a couple of weeks in office his approval rating has dropped to 43% while his disapproval rate has risen to 53%. There is a lot of talk about impeachment and it also has been gaining approval by voters. Initially 35% supported the idea of impeachment, then it grew to 40% and now it is even with 46% approving and 46% disapproving of the idea.

A recent poll by CNN finds that 53% of Americans oppose Trump's travel ban whereas only 47% favor it. Six in ten Americans oppose his plan to build a wall on the Mexican border.

Seventy four percent of Americans, including 53% of Republicans, believe Trump should release his tax returns. According to a poll at CNN Money, 6 out of 10 Americans feel Trump is not doing enough to avoid conflicts of interest.

The cartoons in this book examine, in a humorous way, some of the problems associated with this presidency. We are hopeful that these cartoons may help lead to better solutions in the future and we feel these cartoons accurately reflect the mood of the majority of American voters.

PART OF TRUMP'S
NATIONAL PARKS PLAN

"Do you solemnly swear to tell the alternative truth, the whole alternative truth, and nothing but the alternative truth....? "

" I'VE JUST BEEN INSULTED BY THAT SO-CALLED PRESIDENT. "

" AFTER TWO YEARS OF VETTING, WE KNOW MORE ABOUT THE REFUGEES THAN WE KNOW ABOUT TRUMP'S FINANCES. "

Gag Idea suggested by Daniel Benjamin

"LIFE WAS SIMPLER IN THE OLD DAYS WHEN ALTERNATIVE FACTS WERE JUST PLAIN OLD LIES."

WHAT HIS STAFF HASN'T TRIED YET TO KEEP TRUMP UNDER CONTROL . . .

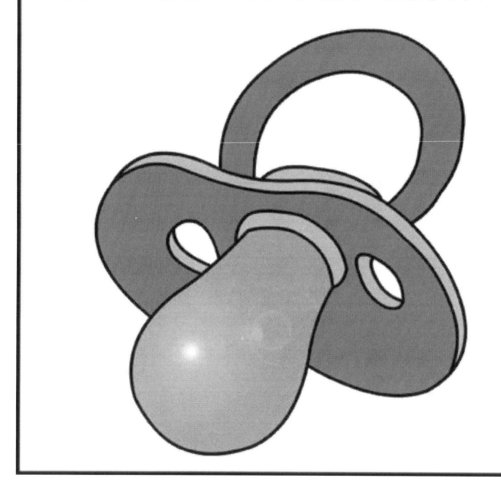

"HE LEARNED HIS DEBATING TECHNIQUES AT TRUMP UNIVERSITY."

" MR. TRUMP ISN'T AVAILABLE RIGHT NOW. HE'S MEETING WITH SOME ENGINEERS FROM BERLIN TO LEARN HOW TO BUILD A WALL. "

" SIR, YOU WILL BE PLEASED TO KNOW WE'RE EXPECTING A LARGER CROWD FOR YOUR IMPEACHMENT HEARING THAN WE SAW FOR BILL CLINTON. "

" MAYBE THIS WILL KEEP HIM FROM STICKING HIS
  FOOT IN HIS MOUTH. "

I would like to thank the following cartoonists and writer for their contributions to this book:

Theresa McCracken

Douglas Blackwell

Cliff Ulmer

Neil Grahame

Christopher Toler

Daniel Benjamin

(And I contributed a few of my own cartoons)

- Ron Coleman

Made in the USA
Charleston, SC
13 February 2017